G. F. Handel

FOUR CORONATION ANTHEMS

HWV 258–261

Vocal Score · *Klavierauszug*

Edited by · *Herausgegeben von*
CLIFFORD BARTLETT

© *Oxford University Press 1988*

Reprinted (with corrections) 1990, 1991, 1992, 1993, 1994, 1995, 1996, and 2001

Oxford is a trade mark of Oxford University Press

Oxford University Press, Great Clarendon Street, Oxford OX2 6DP, England

Oxford University Press Inc., 198 Madison Avenue, New York, NY 10016, USA

*The full score and instrumental parts are also on sale. Full scores, vocal scores, and instrumental
parts are available for hire from the publisher's hire library.*

A list of corrections made in this reprint is available from the publisher's hire library.

PREFACE

George I died at Osnabrück on 11 June 1727, and his successor was proclaimed King as George II on 15 June. The first mention of his coronation was at a meeting of the Privy Council on 11 August 1727. Under normal circumstances it is likely that the music would have been entrusted to the Organist and Composer of the Chapel Royal. But the holder of that position, William Croft, died on 14 August. Maurice Greene, recommended on 18 August by the Bishop of Salisbury as 'the greatest musical genius we have', was appointed on 4 September. Whether Greene expected to compose the coronation anthems is not known, but by 9 September it was known that 'Mr. Hendel, the famous Composer to the opera, is appointed by the King to compose the Anthem at the Coronation which is to be sung in Westminster-Abbey at the Grand Ceremony'. According to a note in George III's copy of Mainwaring's biography of Handel, the King himself insisted that Handel should compose the music instead of Greene. It is possible that the subsequent ill-feeling between Handel and Greene may have been because of this (or because Handel expected to get Greene's job).

The precise order of service was not agreed until a meeting of the Privy Council on 20 September. Until then it had been expected that the service would be on 4 October so it is likely that Handel had already started his anthems. That would account for discrepancies between the texts he set and those in the official order of service, the printing of which (only 100 copies) was authorized at that meeting. Because of the likelihood of flood in the neighbourhood of the Abbey, the coronation was postponed until 11 October. Unusually, Handel did not date his manuscript. *Let thy hand* and *Zadok the priest* both follow the text of the 1685 coronation, which had recently been reprinted; the other two anthems have texts taken directly from the Book of Common Prayer and the Bible. Burney quoted Handel as responding to the receipt of the official texts for him to set: 'I have read my Bible very well, and shall choose for myself.' The fact that Handel quotes the Bible references at the head of the three anthems whose opening pages survive suggests that he did indeed do so.

There are two running orders which may indicate the sequence of events at the service. A copy of the printed order of service survives at Lambeth Palace, with emendations by the Archbishop of Canterbury, William Wake. There is also a list of musical items written in the Chapel Royal Cheque Book by the Clerk of the Cheque, Jonathan Smith. These are printed in parallel in the table opposite. It will be seen that in both lists *Zadok the priest* is the second of Handel's four anthems and *My heart is inditing* the fourth, but that they disagree which of the others came first and third. This edition follows the order in which the anthems now stand in the autograph score. This has no particular authority, since each anthem was originally separate and they were only later bound together, but it is a sensible order for occasions at which all four are performed. Although its original position was mid-service, any audience now will expect *Zadok the priest* to come first and, apart from in an attempt to reconstruct the whole service, there is no reason to disappoint it.

Archbishop Wake's notes suggest that the music did not go smoothly. Apart from the possibility that the Chapel

ORDER OF SERVICE (Wake's annotations in *italic*)	CHAPEL ROYAL CHEQUE BOOK
Procession	O Lord, grant the King a long life Full Anthem (text as set by Child)
Entrance	
Anthem I: I was glad *This was omitted and no Anthem at all Sung . . . by the Negligence of the Choir of Westminster*	I was glad Full Anthem
Recognition	
Anthem II: The King shall rejoice *The Anthem in Confusion: All irregular in the Music*	Let thy hand be strengthened Verse Anthem
Litany	
The Choir singing the Responses to the Organ *To shorten the Service let this be read*	The Litany to be read
Anointing	
Anthem III: Come Holy Ghost *This Hymn by mistake of the Music not sung: but the next Anthem instead of it*	Come Holy Ghost This Chanted for Shortness Sake
Anthem IV: Zadok the Priest	Zadock the Priest Verse Anthem
Anthem V: Behold, O God, our defender	Behold, O Lord, our defender This Chanted
Crowning	
Anthem VI: Praise the Lord, O Jerusalem	The King shall rejoice Verse Anthem
Te Deum	
Anthem VII: We praise Thee, O God *['Anthem VII' deleted]*	Te Deum of Gibbons' was sung
Inthronisation	
Anthem VII: Let thy hand be strengthened [text in full]	
After Homage	
Anthem VIII: The Lord is a sun and a shield	God spake sometimes in visions This Chanted
Queen's Coronation	
Anthem X: My heart is enditing	My heart is inditing Verse Anthem
Communion	
The Organ plays and the Choir singeth: Anthem X: Let my prayer come up into thy presence The Choir sings: Therefore with angels . . . The Choir sings: Glory be to God on high	During ye Offertory the Organ plays, till the Alms are done Collecting Sanctus &c Sung in Musick The Gloria in Excelsis Sung in Musick

Royal choir may not have been of a particularly high standard, there are two plausible reasons: confusion between the rival orders of service and poor communication between the performers. They were disposed on two specially-erected galleries, with sight-lines interrupted by the altar. Subsequently, concerts were advertised as 'The Musick disposed after the Manner of the Coronation Service' (e.g. a performance of *Esther* in 1732), presumably as an attraction, but it may well have proved difficult to control the large forces in such a position.

Handel noted for *The King shall rejoice* the following numbers of singers: 'C[anto] 12; [A. I] H[ughes] et 6; [A. II] Freem[an] et 6; [T.] Church et 6; [B. I] Wheely et 6; [B. II] Gates et 6'. The canto (soprano) part would normally have been sung by boys. But there was a shortage: 5 of the 10 Chapel Royal boys had left with broken voices in June.

This may explain an otherwise surprising reference in *The Country Journal: or The Craftsman* (7 October 1727): 'The Musick composed for the Coronation by Mr. Hendel is to be performed by Italian Voices and above 100 of the best Musicians'. But had the Italian operatic canaries been persuaded to fill the gap, one would have expected some moralist to have condemned it! An account in the *Norwich Gazette* (14 October 1727) dated 7 October reads:

Yesterday there was a Rehearsal of the Coronation Anthem in Westminster-Abbey, set to Musick by the famous Mr. Hendall: There being 40 Voices, and about 160 violins, Trumpets, hautboys, Kettle-Drums, and Bass's proportionable; besides an Organ, which was erected behind the Altar: And both the Musick and the Performers, were the Admiration of all the Audience.

The total of 40 voices is not far from Handel's total of 47; but the number of instruments may be exaggerated a little, however one interprets it (either 160 violins, and other instruments in proportion; or 160 violins, trumpets, etc., and basses in proportion). The complement of royal musicians was 33, and 53 supernumerary musicians were also employed (at three guineas each). Whichever set of figures are taken, though, it is clear that there were significantly more players than singers. The Abbey's own organ was not used: instead one was specially erected by Christopher Shrider at a cost of £130. It was later presented to the Abbey by the King.

There are many references to subsequent performances of one or more of the coronation anthems, though exact titles are rarely quoted. Most of them probably referred to *Zadok the priest*, which has been performed at all subsequent coronations. The anthems were not published until 1743. Unusually, for *Zadok the priest* instrumental parts were issued as well as a full score, and they circulated widely from their inclusion in Walsh's sets of Handel's Overtures. Parts were advertised for the other anthems, but as no copies have survived, they were probably never issued.

This edition corrects various inconsistencies and carelessnesses in Handel's score and modernizes some aspects of notation. Since his intentions are not in doubt, modern conventions are used for accidentals: those in square brackets, and cautionaries in round brackets, are editorial. Complete details of sources and editorial method, notes on performance, and a critical commentary can be found in the companion full score for this edition. A few suggestions for performance are summarized here.

Unless otherwise indicated, the general dynamic level is assumed to be *f*, written only to indicate return to the norm after *p*. Each movement should generally start at a full level (whether *mf*, *f*, or *ff* is usually self-evident), and other dynamics should grow out of the music rather than be imposed on it. *Zadok* has two unusual indications, 'soft' at the opening and 'loud' at b. 23, written only above the continuo part in Handel's manuscript. Rather than indicating a gradual crescendo, these may just be a warning to the organist that the full forces do not enter at the opening.

There are frequent inconsistencies between the notation of ♪♪, ♩♪, and ♪.♪. This edition suggests adjustment to the note values which Handel uses most often in the movement, but in triple time triplet interpretation is often the best solution, whatever the notation. Braces above the stave indicate hemiola cross-rhythms: these often have the effect of slowing movement down by adding stresses rather than simply changing them, and not all parts need be affected. The notated length of the last note of a phrase should often not be taken literally.

If choirs cannot trill, they can manage an approximation with an appoggiatura and a termination (an anticipation of the following note with a lift in the sound before it). Handel notates terminations inconsistently, and the written note values need not be taken literally; when not notated they should be added.

Handel scored some 'solo' lines for two voices, which may be allocated to a semichorus. If women take the soprano part rather than boys, they should also sing these sections.

Much of the historical information above and the table showing the running order are from Donald Burrows's article 'Handel and the 1727 Coronation' (*Musical Times* 118, June 1977, pp. 469–73), with his kind permission.

CLIFFORD BARTLETT, 1988

VORWORT

George I starb am 11. Juni 1727 in Osnabrück, und sein Nachfolger wurde, als Georg II, am 15. Juni zum König ausgerufen. Seine Krönung wurde erstmals am 11. August 1727 in einer Sitzung des Kronrates erwähnt. Unter normalen Umständen wäre wahrscheinlich der Komponist und Organist der königlichen Kapelle mit der Komposition der Musik betraut worden. William Croft, der dieses Amt bekleidete, starb jedoch am 14. August, und so wurde Maurice Greene, vom Bischof von Salisbury am 18. August als „das größte musikalische Genie, das wir haben" empfohlen, am 4. September zu seinem Nachfolger ernannt. Ob Greene damit rechnete, die Krönungsanthems zu komponieren, ist nicht bekannt: am 9. September war jedoch bekannt, daß „Her Hendel, der berühmte Komponist an der Oper, vom König dazu ernannt worden ist, das Krönungsanthem zu komponieren, das bei der Hauptzeremonie in der Westminsterabtei gesungen werden wird." Laut einer Notiz in Georgs III Exemplar von Mainwarings Händel-Biographie bestand der König selbst darauf, daß Händel anstelle von Greene die Musik komponieren sollte. Möglicherweise rührten die späteren Ressentiments zwischen Händel und Greene von dieser Angelegenheit her (oder von dem Umstand, daß Händel erwartet hatte, Greenes Stellung zu bekommen).

Die genaue Abfolge des Gottesdienstes wurde erst in einer Sitzung des Kronrates am 20. September festgelegt. Bis dahin hatte man angenommen, daß der Gottesdienst am 4. Oktober stattfinden würde, und es ist daher wahrscheinlich, daß Händel bereits mit der Komposition der Anthems begonnen hatte. Daraus würden sich die Unstimmigkeiten erklären, die zwischen den Texten, die er vertonte, und denen für die offizielle Abfolge des Gottesdienstes, deren Druck (nur 100 Exemplare) in dieser Sitzung genehmigt wurde, bestehen. Wegen der Wahrscheinlichkeit einer Überschwemmung in der Umgebung der Westminsterabtei wurde die Krönung auf den 11. Oktober verschoben. Gegen seine Gepflogenheit datierte Händel seine Handschrift nicht. *Let thy hand* und *Zadok the priest* richten sich beide nach dem Text der Krönung von 1685, der kurz zuvor neu aufgelegt worden war. Die Texte der beiden anderen Anthems wurden direkt dem Book of Common Prayer und der Bibel entnommen. Burney zitiert Händels Reaktion beim Erhalt der offiziellen Texte, die er vertonen sollte: „Ich habe meine Bibel sehr sorgfältig gelesen und werde die Auswahl selber treffen." Die Tatsache, daß Händel die Stellenangaben der Bibelzitate zu Beginn der drei Anthems, deren Anfangsseiten erhalten sind, zitiert, läßt darauf schließen, daß er dies tatsächlich tat.

Es existieren zwei Programme, die vielleicht die Abfolge der Ereignisse im Gottesdienst angeben. Ein Exemplar des gedruckten Programms des Gottesdienstes ist, mit Berichtigungen vom Erzbischof von Canterbury, William Wake, im Lambeth Palace erhalten. Eine Liste von musikalischen Stücken, geschrieben vom Schatzmeister Jonathan Smith, erscheint auch im Chapel Royal Cheque Book (vgl. S.ii).

Man wird sehen, daß *Zadok the priest* in beiden Listen die zweite Stelle unter Händels vier Anthems einnimmt, und *My heart is inditing* die vierte, daß sich die Listen jedoch darin widersprechen, welches der anderen Anthems an erster bzw. dritter Stelle stand. Diese Ausgabe folgt der Anordnung, in der die Anthems jetzt in der urschriftlichen Partitur erscheinen. Dieser kommt jedoch keine besondere Autorität zu, da jedes Anthem ursprünglich für sich existierte, und die Anthems erst später zu einem Band zusammengebunden wurden: sie stellt jedoch eine vernünftige Anordnung für Gelegenheiten dar, bei denen alle vier Anthems aufgeführt werden. Obwohl *Zadok the priest* ursprünglich in der Mitte des Gottesdienstes aufgeführt wurde, wird jedes heutige Publikum erwarten, dieses Anthem am Anfang zu hören und es gibt keinen Grund dafür, es zu enttäuschen, außer es handelt sich um einen Versuch, den gesamten Gottesdienst zu rekonstruieren.

Erzbischof Wakes Aufzeichnungen legen die Vermutung nahe, daß die Aufführung der Musik nicht glatt vor sich ging. Abgesehen von der Möglichkeit, daß die königliche Kapelle kein besonders hohes Niveau hatte, gibt es dafür zwei einleuchtende Gründe: Verwechslungen zwischen den zwei rivalisierenden Programmen des Gottesdienstes und schlechte Verständigung zwischen den Ausführenden. Diese befanden sich auf zwei speziell errichteten Gallerien, wobei der Altar ihre Sicht aufeinander behinderte. Später wurden Konzerte als „Die Musik in der Art des Krönungsgottesdienstes angeordnet" angekündigt (z.B. eine Aufführung von *Esther* im Jahre 1732), wahrscheinlich als eine Attraktion, aber es könnte gut sein, daß es sich als schwierig herausstellte, die große Anzahl der Ausführenden in einer derartigen Aufstellung zu kontrollieren.

Händel gab für *The King shall rejoice* die folgenden Sängerzahlen an: „C[anto] 12; [A. I] H[ughes] et 6; [A. II] Freem(an) et 6; [T] Church et 6; [B. I] Wheely et 6; [B. II] Gates et 6". Der canto (Sopran) wäre normalerweise von Knaben gesungen worden. Hier herrschte jedoch Mangel: fünf der zehn Knaben der königlichen Kapelle waren im Juni wegen Stimmbruch ausgeschieden. Diese Tatsache mag einen sonst überraschenden Hinweis in *The Country Journal: or The Craftsman* (7. Oktober 1727) erklären: „Die Musik, die Herr Händel für die Krönung komponiert hat, wird von italienischen Sängern und über 100 der besten Musiker aufgeführt werden." Wären jedoch die italienischen opernsingenden Kanarienvögel dazu überredet worden, einzuspringen, so hätte man erwartet, daß irgendein Moralist dies verurteilte! Eine Beschreibung in der *Norwich Gazette* (14. Oktober 1727), die mit 7. Oktober datiert ist, lautet folgendermaßen:

Gestern fand in der Westminsterabtei eine Probe der Königshymne, die vom berühmten Herrn Hendall vertont worden ist, statt. 40 Sänger nahmen teil und etwa 160 Geiger, Trompeter, Oboisten, Paukenspieler und Bassisten proportionsgemäß; daneben wurde eine Orgel gespielt, die hinter dem Altar aufgestellt war: und beide: Musik und Künstler waren der Gegenstand der Bewunderung des ganzen Publikums.

Die Gesamtzahl von 40 Sängern ist nicht weit von Händels 47 entfernt; die Zahl der Instrumentalisten mag jedoch etwas übertrieben sein, wie immer man sie interpretiert (entweder 160 Geiger und andere Instrumente in Proportion dazu; oder 160 Geiger, Trompeter etc. und Bässe in Proportion dazu). Die Zahl der königlichen Musiker betrug 33, dazu wurden 53 außerplanmäßige Musiker engagiert (jeder erhielt 3 Guineen). Welche Zahl man auch nimmt, es ist offensichtlich, daß bedeutend mehr Instrumentalisten als Sänger teilnahmen. Die Orgel der Abtei wurde nicht verwendet, statt dessen ließ man, um £130, von Christopher Shrider speziell eine Orgel aufstellen. Sie wurde später vom König der Abtei geschenkt.

Es existieren viele Hinweise auf spätere Aufführungen von einem oder mehreren der Krönungsanthems, obwohl die genauen Titel selten angegeben sind. Meistens wird es sich um *Zadok the priest* gehandelt haben, das bei allen folgenden Krönungen aufgeführt wurde. Die Anthems wurden erst im Jahre 1743 veröffentlicht. Entgegen der herrschenden Gepflogenheit wurden für *Zadok the priest* neben der Partitur auch Instrumentalstimmen herausgegeben, die durch ihre Aufnahme in Walshs Serie von Händels Ouvertüren in weiten Umlauf kamen. Für die übrigen Anthems wurden Einzelstimmen angekündigt, aber da keine Exemplare davon erhalten sind, sind sie wahrscheinlich niemals erschienen.

In dieser Ausgabe sind verschiedene Unstimmigkeiten und Unachtsamkeiten in der Partitur Händels berichtigt, sowie in einigen Bereichen der Notation Modernisierungen vorgenommen worden. Da in bezug auf Händels Absichten keine Zweifel bestehen, werden Vorzeichen nach modernen Verfahrensweisen gesetzt, wobei die in eckigen und die Warnungszeichen in runden Klammern vom Herausgeber stammen. Alle Einzelheiten zu ´Quellen und editorischer Methode sowie Angaben zur Aufführung und ein kritischer Kommentar finden sich in der zu dieser Ausgabe gehörenden Partitur. Einige Vorschläge zur Aufführungspraxis werden im folgenden gemacht.

Falls nicht ausdrücklich vermerkt, wird vorausgesetzt, daß das allgemeine dynamische Niveau *f* ist, nur dann ausgeschrieben, wenn nach *p* die Rückkehr zur Norm gekennzeichnet werden soll. Jeder Satz sollte im allgemeinen auf vollem dynamischen Niveau beginnen (ob *mf*, *f* oder *ff* versteht sich meist von selbst), wobei dynamische Veränderungen aus der Musik hervorgehen und ihr nicht äußerlich auferlegt werden sollten. *Zadok* weist zwei ungewöhnliche Vortragsbezeichnungen auf, nämlich „leise" zu Beginn und „laut" in Takt 23, die in

Händels Manuskript nur über der Continuo-Stimme stehen. Hierbei wird es sich weniger um die Bezeichnung eines allmählichen crescendo handeln, als vielmehr nur um einen Hinweis für den Organisten, daß zu Beginn nicht mit voller Stärke eingesetzt werden soll.

Es zeigen sich häufig Unstimmigkeiten zwischen der Notation von ♪♪, ♩ ♪ und ♩.♪. In dieser Ausgabe wird eine Angleichung an die Notenwerte nahegelegt, die Händel im Satz am häufigsten benutzt; im Dreiertakt bietet allerdings die Wiedergabe durch Triolen oft die beste Lösung, ganz unabhängig von der Notation. Klammern über dem Notensystem bezeichnen Hemiolen-Kreuzrhythmen: Diese bewirken oft eine Verlangsamung des Satzes dadurch, daß sie zusätzliche Betonungen schaffen, statt diese nur zu verändern, und nicht alle Stimmen müssen von ihnen erfaßt werden. Die notierte Länge der letzten Note einer Phrase sollte nicht immer wörtlich genommen werden.

Wenn sich Triller für Chöre als problematisch erweisen, kann diesem Effekt annähernd entsprochen werden durch eine Appoggiatura und eine Antizipation der folgenden Note durch Anhebung des Klangs vor ihr. Händels Notation von Antizipationen ist uneinheitlich, und die gesetzten Notenwerte müssen nicht wörtlich genommen werden; wo sie fehlen, sollten sie hinzugefügt werden.

Händel setzte einige ‚Solo'-Passagen für zwei Singstimmen, die von einem Halbchor übernommen werden können. Falls der Sopran mit Frauen- statt mit Knabenstimmen besetzt ist, sollten auch diese Abschnitte von ihnen gesungen werden.

Ein Großteil dieser historischen Informationen und die Tabelle mit der Reihenfolge des Programms sind mit freundlicher Genehmigung dem Artikel „Handel and the 1727 Coronation" (*Musical Times* 118, Juni 1977, S. 469—473) von Donald Burrows entnommen.

Übersetzung: Dorothee Eberhardt   CLIFFORD BARTLETT, 1988
und Martin Lauster

ANTHEM I

ZADOK THE PRIEST

GEORGE FRIDERIC HANDEL
HWV 258

After 1 Kings 1:39–40

Keyboard reduction

Soft

sim.

Printed in Great Britain

OXFORD UNIVERSITY PRESS, MUSIC DEPARTMENT, GREAT CLARENDON STREET, OXFORD OX2 6DP

4

6

ANTHEM II

LET THY HAND BE STRENGTHENED

1

GEORGE FRIDERIC HANDEL
HWV 259

Psalm 89: 13–14

14

2

3

ANTHEM III

THE KING SHALL REJOICE

1

Psalm 21: 1, 2, 3, 5

Allegro

GEORGE FRIDERIC HANDEL
HWV 260

2

*Throughout this movement, both ♪♪ and ♩.♪ may be performed ♩ ♪. See note in full score critical commentary.

3

* See full score for Handel's version of A.2 in bb. 214–17.

4

* One first bass should also sing these five notes (see full score).

ANTHEM IV
MY HEART IS INDITING

GEORGE FRIDERIC HANDEL
HWV 261

1

After Psalm 45: 1, 10, 12
Isaiah 49: 23
Andante

Photocopying this copyright material is ILLEGAL.

58

2

* Small stems in this context indicate performance as notated in Soprano, b. 110.

3

* 🎼

4

* Handel originally doubled the first three notes of this entry in
the Tenor part (see full score).

Printed by
Halstan & Co. Ltd., Amersham, Bucks., England